EMBRACE YOUR FREAKNESS

CREATING THE LIFE
FOR WHICH YOU WERE DESIGNED

FRANK KECK

Lisa,
you are the freak
Embrace it!

[signature] STORM 2010

International Standard Book Number: 978-1-59872-719-7

October, 2009

I would like to thank everyone who has made this book possible. This book has been a dream of mine for several years now and it is so very gratifying to have it finished.
Specific thanks to Laura McKnight and Linda Powers, my tireless editors. Ladies, you took my ideas and helped them to make sense in written form. Your efforts to keep me focused have vastly improved this book. To Heather England, for making this book visually appealing, hip, and much more readable—many thanks!

To Melody, Coach Joe, Adam, Tremendous, and Patch, you all have inspired me in so many ways. You have taught me many of the lessons I have the privilege of sharing here.

To Mom and Dad, you made me (literally) and helped mold me by helping me develop my values and beliefs. You both have been such an integral part of my life and I love you so much for being the best parents and role models.

To the Keck family, thanks for your continued love and support. It is very reassuring to know you are always there, in good times and bad, to pick me up or to help me celebrate. Thank you for sharing your joys and sorrows, for allowing me to help pick you up, and for letting me celebrate the joys of life with you.

To Dax and Leo, you are the lights of my life. You are proof to me that God is great. I thank Him every day for the joy and happiness you both bring to your mom and me.

Finally, and most importantly, to my adorable Rachel: You are the love of my life and every day you inspire me to do more and to be a better person. Without you, my life would be empty. With you, I'm fulfilled. You have truly helped me to create the life for which I was designed. I love you.

Frank

CONTENTS

THE PURPOSE OF THIS BOOK

"If one advances confidently in the direction of his dreams, and endeavors to live the life which he has imagined, he will meet with a success unexpected in common hours."
--Henry David Thoreau

Fulfillment—creating the life for which you were designed—that's what it's all about. You might not be able to define fulfillment, but you certainly know whether you have it or not. Have you ever wondered why some people seem to be more fulfilled than others? Do you wonder why sometimes the folks who have nothing seem the most contented, while others who have everything imaginable in terms of success and material comforts still may not be fulfilled?

Have you ever met someone extremely successful yet unfulfilled? I have. In fact, I've met lots of them. Of course, to be fair, I've also met many unsuccessful people who are unfulfilled. I'm sure you know both kinds too.

I believe that life is about creating fulfillment. In order to create fulfillment, however, you must learn to like yourself first, or have self-esteem. Most people know they need self-esteem. In one Gallup Poll, 89% of respondents said that self-esteem was the primary factor for them to work harder to succeed. 63% said that spending time and effort to develop self-esteem was a worthwhile endeavor. Low self-esteem affects people of all ages, colors, races, and ethnicities. It's an epidemic affecting rich and poor alike. Low self-esteem is an equal opportunity offender.

Why do people have low self-esteem? I believe it's because they haven't discovered and embraced their freakness. Your freakness is everything that makes you unique and guides your purpose in life. It's what sets you apart and makes you remarkable. Discovering your freakness is the first step toward learning to like yourself and raising your self-esteem.

So, what are your God-given talents and abilities? What are you really good at doing? What things make you happy? If you didn't have to worry about earning a living, what would you enjoy doing every day?

As I have studied and interviewed happy, fulfilled people, I've found that they share several common elements. Most importantly, they have all solved what I call "The Fulfillment Equation."

The Fulfillment Equation

Take Inventory + Take Aim + Take Care = Take Off!

1. Take Inventory: Take time to discover what things you are inherently good at and what you truly enjoy doing. Figure out who you are so you can discover what you were designed to do.

2. Take Aim: Use what you've learned about who you are to formulate an ideal picture of who, what, and where you want to be. Motivation comes from knowing your purpose in life and then setting out to fulfill it.

3. Take Care: Create a plan to nurture and develop your newfound freakness. Learn how to put the right fuel in your tank so you get the best performance.

4. Take Off: Get ready to start living the life for which you were designed. Now that you know who you are, where you're headed, and how to take care of yourself, you're ready to go from being different to making a difference!

Embrace Your Freakness will show you how to progress through each step of the Fulfillment Equation by putting simple, proven elements into practice in your everyday life. Congratulations on starting your journey toward true happiness and fulfillment!

"Far better is it to dare mighty things, to win glorious triumphs---even though checkered by failure---than to rank with those poor spirits who neither enjoy much nor suffer much, because they live in a gray twilight that knows not victory nor defeat."
--Theodore Roosevelt

1. TAKE INVENTORY
GETTING TO KNOW YOU

"Today you are You, that is truer than true. There is no one alive who is Youer than You."

--Dr. Seuss

"Know thyself."

--Socrates

I was sitting at my desk the other day and thinking . .

You wouldn't pull your camper with a moped.
You wouldn't hunt squirrels with hand grenades.
You wouldn't highlight a book with a black marker.
You wouldn't pick a flower with a lawnmower.
You wouldn't plow a field with a screwdriver.
You wouldn't light a candle with a flame thrower.

You wouldn't do these things, because the tools aren't suited to the intended task. They aren't being used for their proper purpose. That's a no-brainer, right? We get it. Then why do we expect to find fulfillment living a life we weren't designed to live?

When we consider the things that lead to fulfillment, we have to admit that some people are just naturally smarter, harder-working, or better-looking than average, and those things undoubtedly pave their way to success. However, there is one thing that *all* successful, fulfilled people have in common: they have figured out their freakness. They have discovered what makes them unique—their particular interests, talents, and experiences. Then they've figured out how to use these raw materials to fulfill the purpose for which they were designed.

In the movie *City Slickers*, Billy Crystal and two of his male friends, facing their 40th birthdays and experiencing midlife crises, decide they need time away from their "soft" city lives. They set out to vacation at a dude ranch, where they will be responsible for a two-week-long cattle drive through the Colorado Mountains. Along the way the urban cowboys encounter bad weather; macho, gun-wielding ranchers; and pregnant cattle; but they finish the drive with their lives back on track. The expedition is headed up by Curly, a seasoned cowboy played by the late Jack Palance, who has no patience for the city slickers and their large learning curve. In my favorite scene, Palance and Crystal are riding along and talking about the meaning of life. Palance holds up his right index finger and says, "It's about one thing." When Crystal asks what that one thing is, Palance replies, "That's what you have to figure out."

In a nutshell, that's what *Embrace Your Freakness* is all about: figuring out how to make the most of your unique talents and abilities so that you can do "that one thing" you were designed to do.

Figuring Out Your Freakness

What abilities do you have? What are your passions and inclinations? All of us were born into particular life situations with inherent likes, dislikes, personality traits, strengths, and weaknesses. We don't have any control over these things, but we can learn to make the most of what we've been given. Are you using your freakness as it was intended to be used?

Let's start with a definition:

Freakness: *(freek-nes) – n*

> 1. The combination of your individual gifts and talents; 2. The phenomena that make you remarkable and unique, equipping you to fulfill your specific purpose in life.

Figuring out what makes you unique—your freakness—is just the first step in your journey toward fulfillment. Once you've identified your freakness, you have to embrace it, channel it, and nurture it, so that it will enable you to create the life for which you were designed. The process of finding fulfillment is a journey, not a sprint, and you may have to re-read this book at each stage of the process. Use it as a life workbook. Do the exercises with the important people in your life, or with the support of the Embrace Your Freakness workshop. You will need a lot of support and encouragement on your way to living a fuller, richer, and more rewarding life.

Seven Famous Freaks

Not sure you want to embrace your freakness? Here are a few historical examples of individuals who embraced their freakness and went on to lead successful, fulfilling lives:

Leonardo da Vinci – Da Vinci discovered early in life that he had a passion for asking questions and solving puzzles. He probably drove his parents and teachers crazy, but he was able to push the limits of what was understood by his contemporaries, drawing pictures of helicopters and parachutes hundreds of years before technological advances would allow either to be built. It was this curiosity combined with his natural artistic abilities that helped Da Vinci paint the *Mona Lisa* and the *Last Supper*. His father had seen his natural gift for artistry and insisted that young Leo pursue these gifts. Da Vinci took his inquisitive nature, added a passion for creativity and helping others, and became the most creative mind of his time.

Albert Einstein – One story Einstein liked to tell about his childhood was that of a wonder he saw when he was four or five years old: a magnetic compass. The needle's invariable northward swing, guided by an invisible force, profoundly impressed the child. The compass convinced him that there had to be "something behind things, something deeply hidden." It was this sense of wonder that was Einstein's Freakness.

Even as a small boy Albert Einstein was self-sufficient and thoughtful. According to family legend, he was a slow talker always pausing to consider what he would say. His sister remembered the concentration and perseverance with which he would build houses of cards. Einstein's Freakness came from combining his sense of wonder with his perseverance and concentration. Though he flunked 8th grade mathematics, Einstein's passion for following his sense of wonder helped him formulate the theory of relativity, changing the face of modern physics and making Einstein the pre-eminent scientist of the 20th century.

Mother Theresa – Mother Theresa grew up poor and accepted a vow of poverty, yet she enriched the lives of countless people all over the world. In her 45 years of ministering to others, Mother Theresa built over 600 missions in more than 123 countries. By putting others' needs above her own, Mother Theresa inspired people around the world to help the poor and oppressed. Mother Theresa's Freakness (probably not a phrase you thought you would ever hear, is it?) was her ability to put others first. She combined her passion for helping others with a vision for creating better lives for thousands of people.

Steve Jobs – Steve Jobs dropped out of college after taking just one course. But Jobs' lack of higher education didn't affect his ability to imagine new possibilities and to persuade others to embrace his vision and follow his lead.

Jobs became the creative genius behind Apple Corporation, and his company continues to create innovative new products purchased by consumers around the world. Using his imagination to create things that he thinks people need then convincing them those things are needed, that is Steve Jobs' Freakness.

Oprah Winfrey – Oprah started her life on a farm in Mississippi, where she began speaking by reading aloud and reciting books at the tender age of three. After moving around to various homes, and after suffering physical, emotional, and sexual abuse, she moved in with her father and kept looking for ways to help others and to stay in front of her audience. Oprah's two interests—being in front of an audience and helping others avoid the horrors she had experienced as a child—came together to define Oprah's Freakness, which she embraces to this day.

Tiger Woods – Woods started imitating his father's golf swing when he was 6 months old, and appeared on the Mike Douglas show when he was only 2 years old. When his father, Earl, saw Tiger's ability and passion for the game, he coached his son to combine his natural ability with a freakish determination to always do his best. Tiger's Freakness is this desire to always give his best effort, combined with his natural athletic ability and his love for the game of golf.

All these individuals embraced their freakness, whether or not anyone else agreed with their chosen path in life. They had confidence in themselves, and that allowed them to make things happen. If you develop this same confidence, you'll be able to join them in achieving great things in your own life.

Getting Started

The rock band, The Who, ask in a song "Who are you?" If you're like me, you probably grew up living day to day, going to school, playing sports, hanging out with friends, getting your first part-time job, maybe heading off to college, and eventually starting your first full-time job. You did what you needed to do without really pausing to figure out what sort of person you were or where you were headed. For many of us, it takes a midlife crisis to make us take the time to identify our freakness and take stock of who we are and where we want to go with our lives.

Let's start with a big question: are you a "wandering generality" or a "meaningful specific?" Well-known motivational speaker Zig Ziglar defines a wandering generality as someone who wanders through life without any specific purpose, whereas a meaningful specific is someone who knows where they are headed at each point along the trail. Obviously, you'd rather be a meaningful specific, knowing who you are and what you stand for. In order to become a meaningful specific, you need to discover your unique gifts and figure out what you're supposed to do with them, i.e., realize your purpose in life.

Discovering your unique gifts, your freakness, involves looking at your entire life, examining what you've done up to this point, figuring out what you've liked, disliked, excelled at, been lousy at, pursued, and avoided. There are a lot of exercises to help you. Go with your gut, and write down the first thing that comes to your mind unless the directions tell you to do otherwise. The more thorough and thoughtful your answers, the more precisely you'll define the freakness that makes you you.

Childhood

In order to get at the real you, we need to go back to your childhood. What kinds of things did you do as a kid? How did you like to spend your time? What sort of friends did you seek out? To what activities/events did you look forward, and what activities/events did you do anything you could to avoid? The following questions are designed to help you get a good sense of who you were as a child. You may want to think of yourself at a particular age—6, 8, 10—as you answer. Take some time to go through all of the questions and answer them as completely as you can.

List five things you did for fun when you were a child.

1. _____

2. _____

3. _____

4. _____

5. _____

Did you prefer playing inside or outside?

How would you have completed this sentence?
When I grow up I want to be ...

_____

_____

What did people say you were good at doing?

_____

_____

_____

What kinds of things did you daydream about?

_____

_____

_____

Which cartoon character best described you as a kid?

_____

_____

What did you like best about that character?

_____

_____

I have read in articles on the internet that the character you chose, and what you like most about them, is how you see yourself. I have found this to be fairly accurate and usually a lot of fun when you do it with other people.

Circle all that apply and add your own:
When I was a child, I enjoyed:

playing cops and robbers	mowing lawns	dodge ball	dolls
playing doctor/nurse	video games	red rover	trucks
duck, duck, goose	Simon says	tetherball	soccer
guns/weapons	Frisbee®	jump rope	golf
stuffed animals	watching TV	board games	baseball
having lemonade stands	hide and seek	playing cards	hockey
steal the bacon	paper routes	swimming	tag
bullying other kids	football	superheroes	jacks
twenty questions	surfing	hopscotch	
imaginary friends	curling	basketball	
playing house	kick the can	computers	
riding my bike	four square	marbles	
capture the flag	bowling	tennis	

What things did you not like doing?

_____

_____

Who was your favorite family member? (aunt, uncle, brother, sister, etc.)

_____

_____

The Teenage Years

Now we'll move onto your teenage years. While some people did not change much between childhood and adolescence, others changed quite a bit.

When I was a little kid, I was very outgoing and loved to ride my bike on obstacle courses set up in the vacant lot next to our house. I would ride for hours, not stopping until it was too dark to see where I was going. (There were no street lights in our neighborhood in those days.)

As a teenager, we moved closer into town, and my interests changed. I was more into running and playing music. I left my love for bike riding and obstacle courses behind.

As you think about your teenage years, think about how you were the same or different from when you were younger. The goal of these questions is to spur your memory, to help you remember both the good and the bad of your teenage years.

When you were a teenager, what did you do for fun?

_____

_____

Did you prefer to spend time inside or outside?

Did you like spending time by yourself, with one or two friends, or with lots of friends?

_____

_____

Who was your best friend as a teenager?

_____

What did you like best about that person?

_____

_____

What was your favorite subject in school?

_____

_____

What was your opinion of school?

_____

_____

How would you have completed this sentence, When I finish high school I want to be ...

_____

_____

What did people say you were good at doing?

_____

_____

What kinds of things did you daydream about?

_____

_____

Adulthood

Now that we've dealt with the past, let's move into the present. Please answer the following questions based on who you are today:

What is your favorite animal?

What is your favorite color?

What is your favorite number?

What kind of movies do you like?

What types of books do you like to read?

List five people you enjoy hanging out with:

1. _____

2. _____

3. _____

4. _____

5. _____

Name the five people who have taught you the most in life:

1. _____

2. _____

3. _____

4. _____

5. _____

**Awesome Bonus Materials
Available Online
embraceyourfreakness.com**

If you were to create a personal slogan, what would it be? (such as "Do unto others as you would have them do unto you," "Leave them better than you found them," "Do it right the first time," or the popular saying from the stand up comedian, Larry the Cable Guy, "Git 'R' Done.")

Name five things that make you remarkable: (The definition of remarkable is to cause someone to make a remark. So what is it about you that would make other people comment about you?)

1. _____

2. _____

3. _____

4. _____

5. _____

What do people notice about you?

_____

_____

_____

What do you most love to do?

_____

_____

_____

What has always come naturally to you?

_____

_____

_____

What do you love to learn about?

_____

_____

_____

Name five traits you admire in others:

1. _____

2. _____

3. _____

4. _____

5. _____

Name three things that set you apart:

1. _____

2. _____

3. _____

Name something that has always grabbed your attention:

_____

_____

_____

What makes time stand still for you?

_____

_____

_____

Name something at which you excel:

_____

_____

_____

What things in life give you positive energy, make you feel great, energized, like you could do anything?

_____

_____

_____

List five words others would use to describe you:

1. _____

2. _____

3. _____

4. _____

5. _____

How would you describe your personality?

_____

_____

_____

List your three biggest accomplishments to date:

1. _____

2. _____

3. _____

List three things you would like to accomplish before you die:

1. _____

2. _____

3. _____

Whew! Well done. You have just written down quite a few things about yourself. Now, let's look at what you wrote. What does it say about you? What does it tell us about your freakness?

When I was trying to find my Freakness, I did many of these same exercises. When I had gathered all of this information, I looked at it and said to myself, "Now what?"

A friend of mine suggested that I look at all of this information about myself and start to look for trends and patterns. What things have you gravitated towards consistently, through childhood, adolescence, and adulthood? What similarities do you see in things you avoided as a kid, as a teenager, and even as an adult? When I started looking for patterns in my life, I noticed a few right off the bat. First, I was funny. I could make people laugh, and I really enjoyed it. Second, I was funny looking, or at least some of the kids I went to school with had convinced me I was funny looking. Kids can be cruel.

I also noticed I did not like doing things that everyone else was doing. I liked to be independent in my thoughts, but I liked to be around people. I could be alone and be happy, yet I liked being in groups as well. Funny, as a motivational speaker, you spend time in front of the audience and then you spend quite a bit of time alone preparing material—a combination that fits me to a T.

I also noticed that I was shy in front of the girls that I thought were cute. This was a challenge for me right up until I met my wife, Rachel. I was so wowed by her that I overcame my fear of beautiful women, and eventually, I asked her out. The rest is history.

The lesson in all this is that you can utilize your strength patterns, and you can overcome your weakness patterns. Take a break, go outside and enjoy the weather (whatever it is) and come back in an hour, or in a day, and start looking for patterns in your life.

Talents

Talent: [tal-*uh* nt] – n

> 1. A special natural ability or aptitude. 2. A capacity for achievement or success.

Talents—everyone has them. Some of you probably have a wide range of talents in a variety of areas, while others have one or two highly developed talents in a single area. Your talents are the raw material you bring to life, the building blocks of your freakness. When you embrace your freakness, you develop your talents into the specific skills and abilities that will enable you to live the life you were designed to live.

My brother-in-law, Mark, is an amazing musician. When he was in his mother's womb, his father sang to him and played musical instruments for him, and, when he was a young boy, he was a musical prodigy. He learned to play the piano at age five and began writing music at age seven. Growing up, he honed his enormous musical talent and became a world-class musician and composer. He also became a very successful jingle writer. You may have heard some of the catchy tunes he wrote for Bud Light, Oldsmobile, and Doublemint Gum. When I asked Mark to write some music for my wedding, he sat down and hammered out an absolutely spectacular piece of music in about ten minutes.

Mark is a great example of someone who is both successful and fulfilled because he has discovered how to use his talents to live out his purpose in life.

When I was 18, I learned that it's not a good idea to compare your talents to anyone else's talents. I went to see my first motivational speaker, Zig Ziglar, at Kiel Auditorium in St. Louis, Missouri. It was awesome! He had 10,000 people all stirred up—cheering, laughing, even crying. I had never seen anything like it. Zig made me feel like I could do anything . . . until I made the mistake of comparing myself to him.

Obviously it wasn't a fair comparison. I was comparing an eighteen-year-old college freshman, whose only speaking experience came from entertaining his family at the dinner table, to the world's best motivational speaker, a man who traveled the world motivating and encouraging other people. It would take me ten years to get up the nerve to consider speaking as a profession and another ten to actually start doing it. I had no business comparing my eighteen-year-old self with a man who had been honing his speaking skills for more than ten years.

When you're exploring your talents, don't make the same mistake I did. Don't put yourself at a disadvantage by comparing yourself to others. Your talents are uniquely your own. They are what make you special, remarkable, awesome. Concentrate on what you were designed to do; don't worry about whether or not you can do it as well as someone else. Take a moment to think about all the talents you possess.

List at least ten of them here:

1. _____

2. _____

3. _____

4. _____

5. _____

6. _____

7. _____

8. _____

9. _____

10. _____

One of my talents is my ability to make people laugh. When I was a kid, I would liven up family meals by making my brother Tom laugh at the dinner table. On a particularly good night I could make Tom laugh so hard that his milk would come out through his nose.

Making people laugh wasn't something I had to work at—it just came naturally. As I've gotten older, I've honed this talent so that it's a reliable skill and a regular feature of my programs. To this day, Tom will not drink milk when we're together for a meal.

Now go back over your list of talents and put them in order, with the strongest as number 1.

Skills

Skill: /skɪl/ Pronunciation Key [skil] – n

> 1. The ability to do something well. 2. An ability arising from knowledge, practice, or aptitude.
> 3. Competent excellence in performance; expertness; dexterity.

Skills are a bit different from talents. Whereas talents are natural abilities that you're born with, skills must be honed and developed. You might be born with a good ear for music, but you can't become a skilled pianist unless you put in long hours of practice. Sometimes we can develop skills in areas where we're not innately gifted or talented, but that's usually an uphill battle. Even when we have a natural ability in a certain area, it takes hard work to turn a talent into a skill.

My sister Kim was always a great student who excelled at whatever she set out to accomplish. As a child, she was good at a number of different things, but her talent for riding horses really stood out. When Kim went to college, she retired from riding and pursued photography and aviation. Photography came easily to her, just like horseback riding had, but she really had to work at learning all the science and engineering behind aviation. Kim didn't get discouraged though. She worked hard to develop all the skills she would need as a pilot, because she really wanted to make flying her career.

All Kim's hard work paid off. She has been a commercial airline pilot since 1987, and she has a spotless record as one of the top pilots with United Airlines. She has worked her way up the corporate ladder to become First Officer for the Boeing 757. Kim may not have been innately talented at aviation, but she used her talent for being very focused and methodical to learn all the skills she needed to fly gigantic jetliners. (Next time you are on a United 757, check out the First Officer. If her name is Kim, say hello from me and get ready for a safe and smooth ride!)

As you think about your own skills, try to include both specific skills, like typing 60 words per minute, and general skills, like organizational ability or leadership. Please start by listing ten skills you use every day either at work or at home.

1.	6.
2.	7.
3.	8.
4.	9.
5.	10.

Now think about those more specialized skills that you use only occasionally. List five here:

1.

2.

3.

4.

5.

Are there some skills that you once had but that have grown a bit rusty? If you can think of any skills that might need a bit of polishing, list them here:

1.	6.
2.	7.
3.	8.
4.	9.
5.	10.

Now take a few minutes to look over your lists of skills. Pretend that you are creating a top ten list, with your most highly-developed skill as number 1, on down to your tenth- most-developed skill at number 10. Do your best to rank your top ten skills here:

1.	6.
2.	7.
3.	8.
4.	9.
5.	10.

As you think about what you want to do with your life to make it more fulfilling, you will want to look at all of your talents, skills and abilities to see what patterns start to emerge. Just as you did at the end of the Talents section, do a review here. What patterns can you discern from analyzing your skills? At what kind of jobs would you be good? What do these skills tell you about yourself? Who might benefit if you were able to use these skills?

The "Is the glass half full …" conundrum

"Every path has some puddles."

--Unknown

Are you the kind of person who sees the glass as half full or half empty? Unfortunately, I think too many of us are half empty folks. We focus on the negatives in every situation, never the positives. Whatever the situation, we assume the worst. In some cases, our half-empty approach stems from our childhood. It's learned behavior, and we have to unlearn it. We have to search for the positive in every situation so that we can begin to see all the glasses in our lives as half full.

The same is true of the way we see ourselves, i.e., our self image. Instead of focusing on our strengths—all the wonderful talents and abilities that make us unique and wonderful—we focus on our weaknesses. We sell ourselves short, seeing our lives and our resumes as half empty when we should see them as half full. The exercises you did earlier, identifying your talents and skills, should help you begin to change your thinking. Concentrate on celebrating and developing all the strengths God has given you. Don't tell me what you can't do. Tell me that you can do anything. Remember that success is measured in "cans."

I received some sage advice at a time when I was having a difficult time establishing a lasting relationship. The woman that I was hoping might become my life partner told me that I was "too sensitive" and that she wanted to "just be friends." As all men know, "let's just be friends" is the kiss of death for a romantic relationship. Apparently being sensitive made me a great candidate for a friendship, but not as marriage material. Fortunately, another friend reminded me that sometimes your greatest weakness is also your greatest strength.

My friend was right. My ability to help other people go through difficult times is due to my great talent of sensitivity. I have taken that talent and cultivated it, and now it is one of my top five attributes.

List the things in your life that you perceive to be your five biggest weaknesses:

1. _____

2. _____

3. _____

4. _____

5. _____

Reframing

I had to learn to see my talent for sensitivity as a strength rather than as a weakness—not an easy task when I was feeling rejected. Fortunately, I learned about a powerful tool called "reframing." Reframing is a technique that enables you to take perceived weaknesses and recast them as strengths. Instead of accepting my girlfriend's assessment, I thought about how being sensitive has enabled me to help support many friends through difficult times, how being sensitive has made me a valuable sounding board in times of challenge or crisis. Reframing helped me recast my sensitivity as a desirable ability that I have nurtured and developed into a major strength.

Now look over your list of weaknesses and do your best to reframe them. As you do, you'll take a big step toward seeing your life as half full.

Your five weaknesses reframed:

1. _____

2. _____

3. _____

4. _____

5. _____

Things You Rock At and Things You Stink At

In more than 20 years of speaking and training, I've seen more than my share of successful, fulfilled people. All these people have one thing in common: they do what they love and they love what they do. One of the goals of this book is to get you to the point where you can have that same kind of fulfillment. In order to get there, you need to spend some time identifying things you love to do.

When you're thinking of things to put on your 'love to do' list, don't worry about choosing things you're good at—just list things you truly love doing. For example, I love ironing, and I happen to think I'm pretty good at it, but who's measuring that? I also love to meet new people, and I love helping others. I enjoy being the center of attention, and I love to make people laugh. If you put all those things together you get the job description for a motivational speaker. And one of the perks of my job is that I have to iron my clothes every day so I look the part!

Now list at least ten things you love to do:

1. _____

2. _____

3. _____

4. _____

5. _____

6. _____

7. _____

8. _____

9. _____

10. _____

Good job. You can always add more. I hope you noticed how just thinking about things you love to do is energizing and uplifting. Imagine if you could actually do something you love doing every day!

Now shift gears a moment and think about things you really don't like doing. These are the things that end up on the bottom of your to do list time after time. For example, as a big picture person, I hate paying attention to details;

fortunately, my wife Rachel is awesome at it. So, whenever possible, I leave the details to Rachel and focus on the big picture. It's a partnership that plays to both our strengths.

Now list at least 10 things you do not like to do:

1.	6.
2.	7.
3.	8.
4.	9.
5.	10.

Not only will this list tell you what to stay away from, if you take time to reframe these items, you can identify opposite things you do like doing. For example, I hate to stay in one place. Reframing that, I can say that I love to travel. Reframing your list of things you don't like doing can often help you add to your 'love to do' list.

Things you do not like to do—reframed:

1.	6.
2.	7.
3.	8.
4.	9.
5.	10.

Five Big Failures

"Success is the ability to go from one failure to another with no loss of enthusiasm."

--Sir Winston Churchill

Everyone experiences failure at some point in life. Most of us have failed more times than we can count. But we shouldn't regard our failures as occasions for criticizing ourselves; we should see them as opportunities for learning. If we can figure out what caused us to fail, we can avoid making the same mistakes in the future. With that goal in mind, list your five biggest failures in life.

1. _____

2. _____

3. _____

4. _____

5. _____

Now think about what caused you to fail in each case and what you did to overcome your failures. You're still here, still kickin', so what did you do to bounce back after each failure? Think about the skills and strategies that you used to adapt and adjust after failing. If you haven't included these skills in your skill inventory, go back and add them now.

Ten Great Accomplishments

"Every day you may make progress. Every step may be fruitful. Yet there will stretch out before you an ever-lengthening, ever-ascending, ever-improving path. You know you will never get to the end of the journey. But this, so far from discouraging, only adds to the joy and glory of the climb."

--Sir Winston Churchill

I think Churchill was on to something. Life is about the journey. It is about how you get there. We must celebrate our successes, no matter how big or how small. I have met many people who can tell you in a jiffy their weaknesses. It takes a bit longer for them to tell you a few of their strengths.

This is because as a society, we tend to focus on the negative. Our society is a what-have-you-done-for-me-lately society. Now is the time to change that perspective.

We cannot change society, but we can change ourselves and our view of ourselves. This next exercise is one of my favorites. What I like about it is the focus on what we have accomplished.

I achieved one of my greatest accomplishments when I was 29 years old. I had set a goal when I was 27 to become a Dale Carnegie Course instructor. This was a two-year process and something that I knew would change me. (Interesting how the events in our life change who we are and where we end up.) I studied and practiced for two years, teaching as many classes as I could and really working on the techniques we had been taught.

Then, it was time for the big test. I had worked hard through two years of studying and paid a huge testing fee. Now it was time to see if I had what it took—if I had the right stuff.

This test took 3 weekends, 3 days each weekend. It was almost a month long test! I remember being scared, being excited, being challenged. I remember rising to the occasion, really focusing on what I wanted to accomplish. My mind was set on succeeding, on getting that certificate. At the end of the third weekend, they announced the names of the people who had passed the test to become instructors. "Frank Keck, congratulations" I heard from the Instructor Trainer. My name was one of seven announced that day.

I remember the elation, the joy, the temperature of the blood in my veins getting hotter. I could feel every ounce of blood as it circulated throughout my body. Everything moved in slow motion. I had a three-hour drive back home, but I could have run home on air.

As I look back on this experience, it changed me forever. First of all, I got to teach a class that had changed my life. I now could help others change their lives. Second, it pushed me beyond what I thought I could do; it helped me set new boundaries for what challenges I could take on in life. And third, it gave me a new thrill, feeling the endorphins crank through my body. Doctors say it is the same as if you were to take morphine. Runners high it has been called.

When you create your list of accomplishments, I want you to go back over your life and think about the things that made your blood run hot. What made you so excited that you felt you could walk on air? What gave you the thrill of a lifetime, not simply the joy of accomplishment, but the satisfaction of meeting each challenge along the way? And finally, what changed who you are, to help you become a better you?

Now list 10 great accomplishments. These are things that you had to work at and that were huge victories at the time.

1. _____

2. _____

3. _____

4. _____

5. _____

6. _____

7. _____

8. _____

9. _____

10. _____

Right about now, you are probably saying, "Enough already! This is too much work." In the words of Bill Clinton, "I feel your pain." Take a mind break. Stop thinking for awhile and go do something fun and relaxing for your brain. Go to You Tube and watch some funny videos, or listen to some of your favorite music. Come back to this when you are relaxed and revived.

Passions

passion: [pash-*uh* n] -*n*

> 1. A strong or extravagant fondness, enthusiasm, or desire. 2. A powerful emotion or appetite, such as love, joy, hatred, anger, or greed.

Passion is what adds spice, flavor, and excitement to life. Yet many people can't identify their passions. When asked what they're passionate about, they answer, "I don't know," or "nothing," or maybe "retirement." Can you imagine how

dull life would be if we didn't feel any passion—positive or negative—for anything? Whether it's your family, your hobbies, or even a bowl of your favorite ice cream, list some of the things about which you feel passionate in your life:

If your list of passions included any negative ones, take a moment to reframe them into positive passions here:

Gathering Outside Input

When I was 23, I took a class that was amazingly helpful in developing my self-confidence. After the class had been together for several weeks, we did an exercise that required us to break into small groups and take turns enumerating the strengths and talents we saw in each another. The idea was to get a fuller picture of ourselves by finding out how others saw us. I learned through that exercise that gathering outside input can be extremely useful in getting a clear, complete picture of our unique talents and skills.

In my small group, I listened as my classmates took turns describing the amazing talents they could see in each other. I was struck by how accurate and insightful my classmates were in identifying each others' talents and abilities. In case after case, they were right on target in pinpointing each person's particular abilities and skills.

Nonetheless, when it came to my turn, I couldn't believe they were talking about me when they said I was funny, helpful, caring, thoughtful and intelligent. That wasn't at all how I saw myself. Yet, why would they lie about me, when they had been so accurate and truthful in inventorying everyone else's talents. My classmates not only boosted my self-esteem that day, they also gave me my first glimpse of my freakness. I had no idea that my life would never be the same.

The Outerview: Finding Out How Others See You

Everyone has experienced an interview at one time or another. Employers interview prospective employees in an attempt to figure out how well the interviewee's skills match the job description, or parents interview potential babysitters to find out how prepared the sitter will be to meet their children's needs. When you're being interviewed, you want to enumerate your qualifications, to sell yourself. An interview is a chance to toot your own horn.

An Outerview is a bit different. Instead of tooting your own horn, you're inviting others to toot it. You're inviting people from different areas of your life to provide a detailed picture of your strengths and weaknesses, to share their sense of who you are. As you prepare for your Outerviews, pretend you are Mike Wallace and you need to find five people who will give you the scoop on you.

This should get you started in seeing yourself a little differently, through other people's eyes. It is so important to get other people's input. They see you differently than you see yourself. We all see the world through our own filters. Getting input from different people will benefit you in all areas of life.

Here are your Outerview questions:

1. What are three words that best describe me?

2. What do you see are my greatest strengths?

3. What do you see are my biggest weaknesses?

Now go and pose these questions to five people you know and respect. Record their responses below:

Outerview #1   Name:

1.

2.

3.

Outerview #2   Name:

1.

2.

3.

Outerview #3   Name:

1.

2.

3.

Outerview #4   Name:

1.

2.

3.

Outerview #5   Name:

1.

2.

3.

The Big 50

Think about all of the work you have done so far. Whew! You have done more in-depth self examination than most people will do their entire lives. You should now know yourself better than you ever have. This feeling is, I hope, a bit intoxicating and a bit mind-numbing. To truly know yourself, write down the first 50 words that you can think of that describe you. These can be words that you have come up with in previous exercises, or they can be words that just come to you when you try to describe yourself. They can be words from your Outerviews too. Just get to number 50.

Here are the first few based on the fact you have come this far: winner, tenacious, and dedicated.

Now, write out 50 words that describe you:

1. _____

2. _____

3. _____

4. _____

5. _____

6. _____

7. _____

8. _____

9. _____

10. _____

11. _____

12. _____

13. _____

14. _____

15. _____

16. _____

17. _____

18. _____

19. _____

20. _____

21. _____

22. _____

23. _____

24. _____

25. _____

26. _____

27. _____

28. _____

29. _____

30. _____

31. _____

32. _____

33. _____

34. _____

35. _____

36. _____

37. _____

38. _____

39. _____

40. _____

41. _____

42. _____

43. _____

44. _____

45. _____

46. _____

47. _____

48. _____

49. _____

50. _____

Top Gun

In the movie *Top Gun*, Tom Cruise and Anthony Edwards play two Navy fighter pilots, Maverick (Cruise) and Goose (Edwards). Maverick is the pilot and Goose is his navigator. Both are really good at what they do—the best of the best.

Well, the Navy has a school to help the best of the best become even better. This school is called Top Gun. With this concept in mind, it's time for you to determine the best of your best. Top Gun asks you to identify your top qualities in life.

What is a quality? A quality is any positive attribute. It might be a talent, a skill, a passion, or ability. Heck, it might be a combination of all four.

The goal here is to help you narrow down your greatest attributes, your top qualities in life. So review your Big 50 list and pick your favorites.

List your top five qualities:

1. _____

2. _____

3. _____

4. _____

5. _____

List five qualities you would like to develop:

1. _____

2. _____

3. _____

4. _____

5. _____

These are your Top Gun qualities, the best of the best. After you write these down, let them sit overnight, to marinate so to speak. Look at them again at least 24 hours later. Make any necessary adjustments.

Now that you have your Top Gun qualities, you have a better idea of what your top qualities are so that you can start thinking more about how you can use them to better not only your life, but the lives of other people as well.

**Free Templates
Available Online**
embraceyourfreakness.com

Recap

Amazing how much talent and ability you have, isn't it? Sometimes we overlook our strengths and just focus on our weaknesses. Focus on your strengths, and you can accomplish anything you set your mind to accomplish.

What have you learned so far about yourself? When you review all of your qualities, what new information have you discovered and what insights have you reaffirmed? (Remember, we are focusing only on strengths here.)

What have you learned about the self-discovery process? I realize this is a very general question. Think about the process. What things were easy? What things were difficult? What things did you enjoy and what things were tough? What suggestions would you give others in their pursuit of their Freakness?

2. TAKE AIM
Identifying Your Purpose

""You have brains in your head. You have feet in your shoes. You can steer yourself, any direction you choose."

--Dr. Seuss

Identifying Your Purpose

Many people don't take time to figure out their purpose in life. They just go from day to day without any sense of direction or destination. Does that sound like you? Do you know why you were put on Earth? Do you know what you are supposed to be doing every day? The second step in creating the life you were designed for is to discover what your purpose in life truly is.

I went to my first National Speakers Association meeting in 1998. I was a neophyte speaker, still wet behind the ears. After registering, I was in the hall when a smartly-dressed man walked up to me and introduced himself. His name was Willie Jolly, and, boy, did he fit his name. He was very happy, very positive, and very outgoing. He welcomed me to the convention and asked me to tell him a little about myself. As we talked, one of Willie's questions stumped me, painfully so, because I had no answer for him. I didn't know how to respond when Willie asked, "So, Frank, what do you speak on? What are you all about? What are you passionate about?"

You'd think that question would be easy to answer—after all, I had had several successful speaking gigs by that time. Yet all I could come up with was something like, "Uh…lots of stuff." Of course Willie challenged me. He said, "Frank, to be an effective speaker, you have to know what your passion is, what you care about more than anything. Could you answer that question? What is burning in your gut? How can you go out and make a difference in the world?"

It would take me four years and a lot of soul-searching to come up with a satisfying answer to Willie's seemingly simple question. Now that you've identified your freakness, you are ready to start thinking about your purpose. What do you have a burning desire to accomplish with your life?

Creating Your Personal Core

"Your vision will become clear only when you can look into your own heart. Who looks outside, dreams; who looks inside, awakes."
                                --Carl Gustav Jung

In my seminars, I ask people the question, "What are you all about? Why do you exist?" Most people just look at me like a calf staring at a new gate---in total bewilderment. Most people I have met do not sit down and think about the direction of their life. These are the same people who do not know the difference between a task and a result. A task is something you do in order to achieve a result. Many people confuse the two. Many more people live their lives being task-oriented rather than being results-based. They live day to day, not understanding why they cannot get ahead in life. They don't realize that they have no vision, no purpose, no results about which they are passionate enough to achieve.

To truly be fulfilled in life, you must know why you exist and where you are headed. You must have the roadmap to get there, and you must know your boundaries of what you will do and what you will not do to reach your goal.

What is it that gives your life meaning and substance? What is it that will make your days more fulfilling and joyous? The answers to these questions lie within your Personal Core. Your Personal Core consists of your Vision, your Mission, and your Values statements. When you identify your Personal Core, you create a focused statement of what your life is all about.

Let's look in more detail at the three elements that make up your Personal Core.

Vision: [vi-zhun] —*n*

> 1. What you want to become; what you are working toward; a purpose, a result. 2. The big picture; the gold at the end of the rainbow.

Mission: [Mi-zhun] —*n*

> 1. How you will achieve your Vision; the tasks you will need to accomplish along the way. 2. The road map to the gold.

Your mission in life will consist of all the tasks you need to do to accomplish your Vision, your purpose. Your mission will change throughout the years as your life changes and your talents and skills change.

Values: [val-yooz] -*n*

> 1. The ideals, customs, and beliefs that shape your view of life.

Think of your Personal Core this way: Your Vision is where you are headed, your Life target. Your Mission is how you will get there, your road map. Your Values define your parameters, the lines you won't cross to get to your target.

So where does your Personal Core come from? Here are some tools for you to use that will help you get started in putting together the elements that make up your Personal Core.

When an athlete prepares for an athletic event, he or she does warm ups. This is to get the blood circulating and to make the performance safer and better. We will do the same here before we create your vision, mission and values statements. We will do a few warm up exercises to get the blood flowing in your brain, to get you focused on some of the things you need to get focused on to define your Personal Core.

Some of these exercises may seem similar to exercises you did in the first portion of the book. Whereas those exercises helped you to identify your qualities, these are designed to help you find out what you are about and where you are headed. We will utilize this information later on in this segment of your journey.

My wife reminded me that Socrates said, "The unexamined life is not worth living." That is so true, yet examining our lives can sometimes be painful—especially if we don't like what we see. Nonetheless, taking time to examine where we are and what we're doing is necessary if we want either to affirm where we're headed or to begin moving confidently in a different direction. So, press onward. You'll be glad you did.

"We shall not fail or falter; we shall not weaken or tire. . . . Give us the tools and we will finish the job."

--Sir Winston Churchill

The INNERVIEW

These questions are designed to help you get started thinking a little bit more about who you are and what your Personal Vision Statement will be. Just answer these questions as honestly as possible. Take your time. These are not easy questions. They are designed to make you think.

1. What is your name? Do you have a nickname? What is the origin of your name?

2. Describe your family. Who is in it? What are they like?

3. What are your hobbies and interests?

4. What is your slogan or motto by which you live your life?

5. What is your therapy? What do you do to get away from it all and relax?

6. If you could change one thing about yourself, what would you change?

7. What do other people tell you your greatest strength is?

8. If you left the earth tomorrow, what would people miss the most about you?

9. What is the hardest lesson you have ever learned?

10. What would you try if you knew you could not fail?

11. If you could do five good deeds that could change the world, what would they be?

    1.
    2.
    3.
    4.
    5.

12. If you could have dinner with any three people, living or dead, who would they be and why?

    1.
    2.
    3.

13. What are the four most important values by which you live your life?

    1.
    2.
    3.
    4.

14. What is one piece of advice you want to pass on to others?

15. What are five dreams you have?

    1.
    2.
    3.
    4.
    5.

Look back over your answers and draw a logo or shield that represents the person you just "Innerviewed." Don't worry about your artistic ability. It's your creativity of thought that matters. The only words you can use are your name. Otherwise, you must use pictures to show what you are all about.

My Personal Logo/Crest:

Letters from the Future You

In 1985, the movie *Back to the Future* came out. This movie was one of the biggest blockbuster movies of the year. The story is about our hero, Marty McFly, played by Michael J. Fox, the all-American boy who takes an interest in others and works at making win/win situations. Marty goes back in time by accident (in a sports car no less) and meets up with his parents who have not yet met.

While Marty is trying to get back to the future where his girlfriend is awaiting his return (they have a big date planned), he runs into the town bully, Biff Tannen, played by Thomas F. Wilson. Biff is out to lie, cheat, steal, cajole and push his way to success. He is extremely self-centered and makes people do things he wants them to do with no regard to what they want.

Which character do you think added more to the world? Which one only took from the world?

Your job in this section is to write yourself (and your grandchildren) two letters from the future. In the first one, you'll imagine you lived your life like Biff Tannen—taking whatever you could get from the world and never giving anything back. In this letter, imagine that you never embraced your freakness, never fulfilled your life purpose, and remained a wandering generality. Tell your grandchildren what kinds of things you did, what broken dreams you had, and what things you'd do differently if you could do them over. Be as specific as possible. Imagine that you want to help your grandchildren learn from your mistakes.

Your Biff Letter

In your second letter, you'll write from the Marty McFly perspective. You'll imagine that you embraced your freakness, fulfilled your life's purpose, and added value to other people's lives. Tell your grandchildren what kinds of things you accomplished, what goals you achieved as specifically as possible. What advice would you give your grandchildren to help them live lives as fulfilling as yours has been?

Your Marty Letter

Now that you have completed your Innerview and your Biff and Marty letters, we're going to take your ideas and create a Personal Vision Statement. This statement will help you focus your energies and evaluate possible choices for the rest of your life. It will serve as the guiding ideal directing you toward who you were designed to be and what you were designed to do.

Your Vision Statement

"Vision without action is a daydream; action without vision is a nightmare."

--Japanese proverb

A Personal Vision Statement sums up your big picture dream of what you want, overall, in life. It should be results-based and broad enough that it won't need to change for the next twenty years. It should be simple enough to be understood by a third grader and memorable enough to be remembered by a second grader. Most importantly, your Personal Vision Statement should answer those questions Willie Jolly asked me many years ago, "What are you all about? What are you passionate about?"

A vision statement can be tough to write, so take time to work through the exercises that follow. After the exercises, you'll create a vision statement specific enough to fit your unique purpose in life, yet general enough that it will enable you to confidently evaluate all the choices you need to make to find fulfillment in life.

Maximizer Idea

Invite two of your closest friends over for a Vision brainstorming session. Share with them what you have learned here and help them to write their Personal Vision Statements at the same time as you write yours.

Writing your Personal Vision Statement

Let's start by taking a look back at your letters from the future.

What kinds of things did you find yourself regretting in your Biff letter?

_____

_____

What things did you wish you'd done instead in your Biff letter? (These things are important to finding fulfillment in life.)

_____

_____

What is the overriding theme in your Marty letter?

_____

_____

When you look at the accomplishments in your life, what patterns do you see?

_____

_____

Your Vision is the overarching big picture of what your life is all about. It is not easy to figure out your Personal Vision Statement, but it sure is great once you do figure it out. Then, for the rest of your life, your decisions are easier to make, you are more confident and sure of yourself, and you will clearly see your direction in life.

What are you all about?

_____

_____

_____

Why do you exist? (Nothing like starting with the easy questions, right?)

_____

_____

_____

What is the big picture result that you would like to bring to the world?

_____

_____

_____

What future do you want to create?

_____

_____

_____

Whom are you serving? On what people do you have an impact?

_____

_____

_____

What results do you provide for them?

_____

_____

_____

Now, wrap those answers up in one general statement, and write it here:

_____

_____

_____

Now, write that same statement to fit the following criteria:

1. A ten year old could understand it.
2. An eight year old could remember it.
3. It is short and catchy.

Here are some sample Vision statements from individuals and companies:

"To leave people better than I found them."
                    --Frank Keck

"To inspire and equip women to reach their potential."
                    --Johanna

"To enhance the lives of those I meet by helping them face all situations with enthusiasm and strength."
                    -- Carter

"To provide people a comfortable, safe and affordable home—and a reason to smile!"
                    --Rob

"Working together, moving people throughout life."
                    --Fox Motor Group

"To be the catalyst for relationships between Baptist Healthcare and our diverse communities."
                    --Baptist Health Outpatient Services

"To make a contribution to the world by making tools for the mind that advance humankind."
                    --Apple

"Providing safe and secure access to what you want."
                    --iBahn Networks

"Exploring the past, illuminating the present, and imagining the future."

                                    --National Museum of Australia

After reading through these examples, look back at the Personal Vision Statement you created on the preceding page. Double check that your version meets all three criteria—a ten-year-old could understand it, an eight-year-old could remember it, and it's short and catchy. If it does, congratulations. You have successfully created a working version of your Personal Vision Statement. If not, congratulations. You have started the thought process and are well on your way towards figuring out what your PVS (Personal Vision Statement) truly is.

Now put this book away for 24 hours. Talk to three people who know you the best and who you trust the most. Tell them what you are doing and ask for their support. Share with them your working model of your Personal Vision Statement, and ask them if they think it fits you. If the feedback you get from several people is "that's not you, dude," then perhaps you might want to work on your Personal Vision Statement some more. Take your time and refine it. Their input is good; your input is better.

Remember that your vision statement is for you, not them, not your spouse, significant other, buddy, pal, dog, cat, business partner, boss or anyone else. It is for you so that you know what you stand for and where you are headed. It's good to get their input, but ultimately your Personal Vision Statement has to represent what YOU want in YOUR life.

Your Mission Statement

"Wisdom is knowing what path to take next. . . .
Integrity is taking it."

                                        --Unknown

Your Mission Statement describes how you achieve your Vision; it is the roadmap to your destination. While you created your Personal Vision Statement to be results-oriented and unchanging over time, your Mission Statement will be task-oriented, and you'll change it to reflect changes in your circumstances. No matter where you are in your life's journey, your Mission Statement should tell you exactly what you need to do, step-by-step, from that point, to make your vision a reality.

Look back at the Personal Vision Statement you created in the last exercise. What are the three or four things you will need to do in order to achieve your vision?

_____

_____

_____

Now you will combine all those things into a single Mission Statement. To help you in this process, go to www.embraceyourfreakness.com and read through some sample mission statements. You'll notice that some mission statements are in paragraph form, while others use bullets. You should choose the format that works best for you.

When I completed a vision and mission seminar for an organization recently, one of the participants told me that she had applied the tools that we had talked about for the organization to her own life. She told me that, as a result, she had clearly identified her purpose for the first time in her 54 years on earth and was ready to make some changes. Within a few months, she left her job of 29 years to pursue a career in teaching. She was on fire to fulfill a lifelong dream and to finally begin doing what she was created to do. Wouldn't you love to feel that kind of excitement in your life?

Clarifying Your Values

What are your values in life? Your Personal Vision Statement and your core values determine who you are and who you will become. They are the skeleton of your life—they provide the framework for everything that you think, feel, and accomplish. Your values determine what you do and how you do it. They determine what goals you set for yourself and how you will go about achieving those goals.

From the list of values below (both work and personal), circle the ten that are most important to you as guides for how to behave or as components of a valued way of life. Feel free to add your own values to this list:

Achievement, Friendships, Physical Challenge, Advancement, Growth, Pleasure, Adventure, Family, Power, Helping, Privacy, Creativity, Service, Honesty, Purity, Variety, Independence, Relationships, Influence, Community, Inner Harmony, Recognition, Competence, Integrity, Status, Religion, Competition, Intelligence, Reputation, Cooperation, Involvement, Responsibility, Accountability, Nature, Tranquility, Security, Knowledge,

Self-respect, Decisiveness, Leadership, Serenity, Democracy, Location, Sophistication, Ecology, Loyalty, Stability, Financial Security, Meaning, Efficiency, Freedom, Ethics, Truth, Excellence, Wealth, Excitement, Wisdom, Fame, Success, Order, Personal Development, Synergy, Autonomy

As far as organizations are concerned, I have read many opinions on how many values are optimal. Some experts recommend as few as four and others are comfortable with up to fourteen. For individuals, I think seven is a good number to shoot for, since that number allows you enough latitude to cover all important areas of your life, yet keeps you focused enough that you are forced to leave out non-essentials. You might start by listing as many values as you can come up with and then start paring down your list.

Creating a Family Core

When Rachel and I got married, we went to Hawaii for our honeymoon. Ah, Hawaii—sandy beaches, crystal clear water, and a great place to sit down and write a Family Core. We put together our own description of what we want our family to be. We wrote a family vision, a family mission, and family values. Now when we need to make a decision, we simply look to our Family Core, and it helps us make clear, insightful decisions.

Awesome Free Bonus Materials
www.embraceyourfreakness.com

Setting Goals

"You measure the size of the accomplishment by the obstacles you had to overcome to reach your goals."
                                   --Booker T. Washington

Now that you've clarified your values and formulated your personal vision and mission statements, you need to set some precise goals that will move you in the direction that you need to go. If you use goal-setting wisely, it can be an extremely powerful tool in helping you live out your life's purpose. The key is setting smart and powerful goals that will work for you.

The first three parts of your Personal Core are now finished. Congratulations! You now know where you're headed, and you have a road map detailing how to get there. Now you must set some specific goals that will allow you to move toward creating the life you were designed to live.

I have found that in life, goals make your attitude better, they make you laugh (with joy) when you achieve them, and they typically bring us all success.

Milt the Scoutmaster

When I was eleven years old, I joined a Boy Scout troop—Troop 7 with Milt the Scoutmaster. Milt was a stickler for details and for goals. He made sure that we had the exact number of tent stakes necessary to get all of the tents put up. He made sure we had the exact change to go through the toll booth on the way to and from the campground. He made sure we wrote down exactly what our goals were.

I have Milt to thank for becoming goal-oriented.

When I first joined the troop, I remember one meeting where Milt took all of the new scouts aside and gave us a goals book. He told us that we needed to set some goals that would help us to reach the rank of Eagle Scout.

Milt was pretty successful in this venture. When I got my Eagle Scout award in 1975, I was part of the 60th straight court of honor at which there was at least one Eagle Scout awarded to a member of our troop. That was over twelve years of thirteen- to fifteen-year-old boys achieving the top rank in scouting. Boys of that age are not really known for their goal-setting abilities. Milt somehow got us all to buy into aiming high, and he worked with us until we achieved our goals.

How did he do it? He believed in it and made us believe in ourselves. He explained to us that if we wanted to get to Eagle, we had to be on a schedule; we had to be at a certain point at each specified time. Milt also got to know us and what was important to us, so he could tie our goals into things that we cared about. Ah, one of my first experiences of being motivated. Who knew?

Milt also knew our personalities. He knew which buttons to push to get each of us to hit our goals. He was aware of what particular things were important to each scout, so that he could stress the importance of each scout's goals specifically to that scout's passions and interests.

Who is your Milt? Who will inspire you to work hard on those days where you do not want to write goals, much less review them? Who will help you brainstorm all of the things you want to achieve? Who will help you formulate your dreams into goals? Who will believe in you so that you will have the confidence to give your best effort in all situations? Who will hold you accountable to the dates and timetables that you set for achieving your goals?

The Bigger Picture

Goals are tremendously powerful things. They can help you become more motivated and more successful; they are the key to finding fulfillment in life. Goals give you a specific target to aim for; they're like the destination you type into your car's GPS (Global Positioning System). Goals also provide important benchmarks against which to measure your progress. Don't forget to celebrate (ice cream, anyone?) as you make progress toward achieving your goals.

I believe goal setting is so important that I recommend you set aside time to work on all of your goals every week. Write them down, read them over, and rewrite them as often as you need to. Look at them every night before you go to bed and when you get up every morning so they're always in the forefront of your mind.

There are four key questions you need to answer as you begin the process of creating smart and powerful goals:

What's your desired result?

Where do you want to be in your life in ten years? Where do you need to be in ten years in order to fulfill your life's purpose—to make your personal vision a reality?

If you cannot see yourself accomplishing your goal, you never will. Later on in the book, in section three, you will learn techniques to visualize yourself achieving your goals.

What's your current situation?

Where are you right now in your life? For example, your goal might be to own your own successful business in ten years. Where are you right now with that? Perhaps right now you are working for someone else, gaining the knowledge, skills and attitudes you will need to reach your goal.

How big is your gap?

What distance will you have to cover to go from where you are now to where you want to be in ten years? How far are you from your desired result? (Don't freak out or get discouraged if your gap is big. We will be building our goals in stages, so it is like the old adage, "How do you eat an elephant?" Answer: "One bite at a time.")

What is your plan of action?

What steps do you need to take to move from your current situation to your desired result? These steps will come in the form of long-range, intermediate-range, short-range, and immediate-range goals, as well as strategies for how you will go about achieving them.

Goal setting is just like planning a family vacation. Let's set our goals for a family vacation using the four questions as our guide:

1. What is your desired result?

When you answer this question, you want to be as specific as possible. The more detailed you can be in your descriptions, the better you'll be able to visualize yourself actually achieving the goal of taking this vacation.

Our desired result is to take our family, four people, by car to Disney World in Orlando, Florida for ten days. We will stay at the most family-friendly hotel available. We will eat dinner at the best family-oriented, family-fun-type restaurants, and we will return with wonderful memories of fun, relaxation, and family bonding.

Now we're getting somewhere. We're starting to become specific in defining our long-range goal. The biggest difference between this goal scenario and most of your goals will be the time frame. Most of your goals will be set out over a ten-year period, or even longer. This vacation will obviously be less than that; it will take place in the next year. We project that we need $2,250 to fund this trip.

2. What is your current situation?

I am married with two children, living in Kansas City. I have a job, and I'm able to save $250 per month towards this vacation. I have two weeks of paid vacation time due to me in the next year from my company. At present we have $500 in our vacation fund for this trip. We have a car which is capable of making the trip.

3. What is your variance gap?

We do not have the necessary money saved up yet, nor do we have the reservations for the hotel, or the tickets for the attractions.

4. What is your plan of action?

Our plan of action must include all the steps that will enable us to reach our long-range goal of taking a ten-day trip, with our entire family, by car, to Disney World in Orlando,

Florida. Our goal includes creating memories that will last a lifetime and will help our family to bond with one another.

In order to achieve these long-range goals, our intermediate goals, to be accomplished over the **next nine months**, include:

1. Saving an additional $1,750 to bring our trip account up to the projected $2,250 cost.
2. Making and confirming our hotel reservations.
3. Getting the car serviced and ready for the long trip.
4. Purchasing tickets for the attractions we have chosen to attend.
5. Making sure our kids are prepared for the long car ride, with activities to keep them engaged and also mentally ready to see Mickey Mouse and all the other characters.

In order to achieve these goals, we will need to accomplish the following short-range goals **within the next 3 months:**

1. Select a hotel by researching all of the hotels that fit our criteria.
2. Determine which attractions we want to attend.
3. Start getting the kids excited about taking a vacation together in the car.
4. Set aside $250/month toward our savings target.
5. Determine the best route to get from our home to Orlando.

So that we can be on time and on target with our short-range goals, we need to achieve the following immediate goals in **the next 30 days:**

1. Determine our criteria for selecting a hotel.
2. Determine the criteria for deciding which attractions to attend.

3. Put aside the first monthly amount of $250 in our trip account.

As you can see, the goal-setting process is the same if you're setting ten-year, or one-year goals. In each case, you need to break down your long-range goals into intermediate, short-range, and immediate goals.

Getting More Specific with Goals

As you can see by our vacation example, you will start the goal-setting process by writing down long-range goals. Long-range goals are those goals you want to achieve five to ten years from today. Your long-range goals will be based on your vision and mission statements. They will represent those final destinations that you'd like to type into your GPS.

Your next step will be to create intermediate-range goals. These are the goals that you want to achieve in the next three to five years. Think about your long-range goals as you formulate your intermediate-range goals. If you want to reach your long-range goals within ten years, where do you need to be in years three through five?

Intermediate-range goals are designed to set you up for long-range success. For this reason, intermediate-range goals will most likely change as you get closer to achieving them. As you work towards your intermediate-range goals, keep evaluating your progress. Where are you in the process of reaching these goals, and what changes do you need to make to stay on track, or even to get back on track if you are not where you need to be?

Next you'll write down your short-range goals. These are the things you need to accomplish in the next one to three years

to move you toward your intermediate-range goals and long
-range goals. Short-range goals will be the building blocks to
help you reach your intermediate-range and long-range
goals. Your short-range goals should describe where you
need to be in one to three years to reach your
intermediate-range goals.

Finally, you will write out your immediate-range goals. What
things do you need to do first? What tools and supplies do
you need for the journey? Your immediate-range goals are
the things that you need to accomplish in the next twelve
months so that you can start focusing on your short-range
goals and working towards your ultimate vision for your life.

Creating SMART & POWERFUL Goals

When we started writing goals in Scouts, Milt made us write
out SMART goals. SMART is an acronym that helps us to
think about the elements of the goal—the particulars of the
goal that we need to think about to increase our ability to
achieve those goals.

The following broad guidelines will help you to set more
effective goals:

Specific	Have you written a complete, detailed, concrete goal?
Measurable	How will you know when you have reached your goal? How will you measure it?
Accountable	To whom will you be accountable for this goal?
Realistic	Is this goal realistic? Can it be done?

Time Frame   What is the specific time in which you will achieve the goal?

After studying goals and successful people for the past 15 years or so, I have added a few extra measures to SMART goals that make them POWERFUL as well.

Positive   Is your goal written in a positive rather than a negative form?

Obstacles   What obstacles might you discover and what's the backup plan?

Win/win   Does your goal create a win/win situation?

Encompassing   Have you developed goals in all eight areas of life? (I will explain the eight areas in the next section.)

Rewards   What's in it for you? How will you celebrate once you've achieved your goal?

Fitting   Does your goal fit with all your other goals, as well as with your personal vision, mission and values?

Urgent   Is your goal something you sincerely care about? Is it something you urgently desire, not just a passing whim?

Level-up   Does your goal challenge you to take your game to the next level?

Goals are one of the primary motivating factors for all people. We get into non-goal-setting ruts at times and we need to keep goals in front of us so we can create the best life possible not only for ourselves, but also for our families, our friends, and our associates.

Well-thought-out goals can make success much easier to achieve, because they help you to see how much progress you have made and how much further you have to go.

Before you start writing out your goals, please read the following section about balancing your life.

Wheel of Life Inventory

I meet people all the time whose lives are unbalanced. They spend a tremendous amount of time and energy developing one or two areas of their lives, while other areas get no attention at all. When I worked at an electronics retailer back in the 1990s, one of the managers, Charlie, told me he would take a pay cut to find a job where he could spend more time with his family. Charlie had gone into management to make more money, but he didn't like what his new position was doing to the quality of his personal life.

How much balance do you have in life? What areas are you working hard to develop, and which areas are you giving short shrift? What sacrifices are you making, and are those sacrifices worth the cost to your quality of life in other areas? What aspects of your life are most fulfilling, and which ones should be on life support?

As you're beginning to formulate long-, intermediate-, short-, and immediate-range goals, it's important to focus on getting your life in balance. A well-balanced life is another key factor in feeling fulfilled. Now is the time to start putting down goals in all areas of life so that you can be more well-rounded, living out your purpose in all aspects of life.

In the next exercise, you'll take inventory of how well balanced your life is right now, at this moment. You'll rate seven areas of your life on a scale of 1 to 10, with 10 on the outer circle, and one in the center.

I've divided a circle into eight equal pie pieces and labeled the pieces Spiritual, Family, Professional, Financial, Physical, Personal Growth, Community, and Leisure.

These are the primary areas of our lives where we should be setting goals. Spiritual is the area of life that has to do with your faith, your beliefs. Is your faith where you want it to be? What do you need to do to make it right? Next is Family. This is the area of your life you share with those who are closest to you. Are those relationships where you want them to be? Could you be a better, more supportive mother, sister, brother, or son? Professional is the area of life in which you make your living. Are you doing what you want to be doing from a career standpoint? What do you need to be doing to get to your dream job and career? In the Financial area, ask yourself if you're making the amount of income that you desire. Are you saving or investing the amount you want to save each month or each year? Physical goals pertain to your body and how physically fit and healthy you are now. Personal Growth is your growth from an intellectual and emotional standpoint. Community

**Awesome Free
Bonus Materials
embraceyourfreakness.com**

includes all the ways you give back to the community. Are you doing things to reach out and help others? In the Leisure area, ask yourself whether you're pursuing your hobbies and interests. Are you relaxing and taking time to enjoy life?

Think about all of these different areas and then fill out the Wheel of Life Inventory as follows:

With the center of the circle representing number one, very unfulfilled, and the outer circle representing ten, extremely fulfilled, put a point in each pie segment that represents how fulfilled you are in that area of your life. After you have plotted your fulfillment level in all eight areas, connect the dots and see what shape you get. Do you see a beautiful round wheel, or a lopsided, flat tire, as in this example:

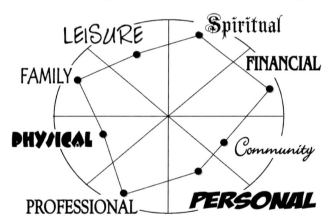

In this example, the person's Spiritual, Professional, Financial and Family goals are in great shape. Physical, Leisure, Personal and Community, however, tell a different story.

I would advise this individual to concentrate more on his/her weaker areas to balance out his/her wheel and to achieve a more well-balanced, well-rounded life. Now use the wheel below to evaluate your own life and to see how well-balanced you are.

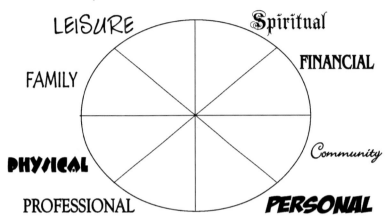

So, how does your wheel look? Is it lopsided? Now is the time to start thinking about all areas of your life, strengthening the weak ones and sustaining the strong ones. You'll want to keep all eight areas in mind as you begin setting your life goals.

Your Bucket List

"If you never did, you should. These things are fun, and fun is good."
-Dr. Seuss

The movie, *The Bucket List*, is about two men who are nearing the end of their lives and want to do several specific things before they die. Using this concept, what are the specific things you want to do before you die? I have broken down your bucket list into different categories, so you don't feel overwhelmed.

Let's start with something simple. Think of ten things you want to do. To get you going, think of at least one for each of the eight different life categories from your wheel of life. For example, I want to visit Australia. I want to meet Seth Godin. I want to read the book *Meatball Sundae*. I want to visit the Great Wall of China. I want to get an article published in *USA Today*. I want to run a 5-minute mile. I want teach my son to read. I want to take my wife on a second honeymoon. I want to save $100,000. Finally, I want to tithe 10% of my annual income to my church.

After you get your first ten, put them into categories. For example, I want to read *Meatball Sundae*. The category for that would be "Ten books I want to read." Here is part of my bucket list as an example:

10 Places to Visit
1. Australia
2. The Great Wall of China
3. All 50 states
4. Disneyland
5. Germany
6.
7.
8.
9.
10.

10 People to Meet
1. Seth Godin (author
2. Bill Self (coach)
3. Oprah(self-made success)
4. Brian Regan (comedian)
5.
6.
7.
8.
9.
10.

10 Books to Read
1. Meatball Sundae
2. The Bible
3. How to Win Friends
4. It Takes 4 to Tango
5.
6.
7.
8.
9.
10.

10 things to teach my kids
1. How to fish
2. How to be confident
3. To have a servant's heart
4. To laugh
5. To eat ice cream
6.
7.
8.
9.
10.

10 Financial Buckets
1. Make $100,000
2. Give away $100,000
3.
4.
5.
6.
7.
8.
9.
10.

10 Buildings to Visit
1. Empire State Building
2. Sears Tower
3. Pyramids
4. Eiffel Tower
5. The Vatican
6.
7.
8.
9.
10.

10 ways to give to church
1. Tithe 10%
2. Time to help others
3.
4.
5.
6.
7.
8.
9.
10.

10 places to get published
1. USA Today
2. Self published
3. A trade journal
4.
5.
6.
7.
8.
9.
10.

10 things that're a blast
1. Ride a roller coaster
2. Drive a Ferrari
3. Ski a black diamond
4. Take Rachel on a date
5. Ride bikes with my kids
6.
7.
8.
9.
10.

10 New Restaurants
1. Luigi's
2. The Mad Hopper
3. Chef Michael's
4. Chez
5. Freebird Burritos
6.
7.
8.
9.
10.

10 Physical Activities
1. Run a 5-minute mile
2. Have 15% body fat
3. Bench press my weight
4. Shoot my age in golf
5. Run a half marathon
6.
7.
8.
9.
10.

10 Events to Attend
1. World Series
2. Final Four
3. Super Bowl
4. America's Cup
5. My kids' graduations
6. My first book signing
7.
8.
9.
10.

These are just some of the things on my Bucket List. You can be more specific or less specific. What things do you want to experience before you die? What is it that you have always wanted to do? Your Bucket List will help you think about what you want to do during your life and that will add life to your years and years to your life. It took me about a month to come up with this number of goals. You may get 50 in one sitting, or you may take much longer. Do whatever works for you. Take your time, do a few each week. Think about the things you really want to do in life. Dare to dream. Think big. Go for it.

My Bucket List by _____

Awesome Bonus Materials

Go to: www.embraceyourfreakness.com
to get free bonus materials
for goal writing and achievement.

Once you have brainstormed your "Bucket List" activities, you determine how to make each one happen. Congratulations, you now have enough to keep you busy for a while!

Goal Origination Action Template (GOAT)

Now that you have thought about the areas of your life, where you need to set goals, along with some of the specific things you want to accomplish with your life, you're ready to write out your goals using the following template:

Goal Origination Action Template (GOAT)

Change Your Goals, Change Your Life

I, _____, do hereby commit to changing my life by changing my goals, which will change my focus, which will change my behaviors, which will bring me fulfillment in life.

My **Specific** goal is:

I will **Measure** this by:

I will be held **Accountable** by:

What makes this goal **Realistic** is:

The **Time frame** for achieving this goal is
_____, which is _____, 20___.

Now check your SMART goal to ensure that it's also POWERFUL:

Positive — Is your goal written in the positive rather than a negative form?

Obstacles — What obstacles might you encounter and what is your backup plan?

Win/win — Does your goal create a win/win situation?

Encompassing — Have you developed goals in the all eight areas of life?

Rewards — What's in it for you? How will you celebrate once you've achieved your goal?

Fitting — Does your goal fit with all your other goals as well as with your values, mission, and vision?

Urgent — Is your goal something you sincerely care about? Is it something you urgently desire, not just a passing whim?

Level-up — Does your goal challenge you to take your game to the next level?

You'll use this template to set goals in each of the eight areas you inventoried above in your wheel of life. Think about the top three things you want to accomplish in each area: Spiritual, Family, Professional, Financial, Physical, Personal Growth, Community and Leisure.

Free Templates Available Online
embraceyourfreakness.com

Ask yourself, "What do I want to have accomplished before I die?" In your Marty McFly letter, you wrote a letter looking back from the future. Review that letter and look at the goals you wrote about, the passions and the dreams. Include these things in the goals you set now.

As you're working on your goals, you should also think about the problems you're facing in your life. What things are causing you to struggle? What do you need to do to overcome those challenges? Think about addressing some of these challenges in your goals.

Developing Your Strategy

Now that you have developed your Personal Vision, Mission and Values Statements as well as your goals, you have to figure out how you are going to fulfill it all.

What is your strategy? What do you need to do? How are you going to do it, and in what order? What tools do you need to make sure you succeed?

Your strategy is how you are going to go about achieving your vision. Your strategy will always be changing; your vision won't.

To develop your strategy, you'll need to know a few things.

Where are you now in relationship to where you want to go? This is a very broad question. The more specific the answer, the better.

Which of the following tools will you need to achieve your Vision?

Knowledge: What knowledge will you need to succeed?

_____

_____

_____

Skills: What skills will you need to succeed?

_____

_____

_____

Attitude: What attitude will you need to succeed?

_____

_____

Resources: What resources will you need, including people, money, and physical resources?

_____

_____

People:

_____

_____

(Be sure to include what it will take to persuade them, or what's in it for them to help you.)

Money:

_____

_____

Physical Resources:

_____

_____

Empowerment: Are you empowered to reach your vision? If not, what will it take for you to be empowered?

_____

_____

_____

Processes: What processes, or procedures, will you need to have in order to fulfill your vision? This might include communication processes, legal procedures, or any type of system, process or procedure that you will need to fulfill your Vision.

_____

_____

_____

Putting It All Together

You've done an incredible amount of work. Now it's time to put it all together. This should start to look like a personal road map to success and fulfillment specifically for you.

Personal Vision Statement:

Personal Mission Statement:

Personal Life Values:

Goals:

Spiritual

> ➢ Long-range
> ➢ Intermediate-range
> ➢ Short-range
> ➢ Immediate-range

Financial

> ➢ Long-range
> ➢ Intermediate-range
> ➢ Short-range
> ➢ Immediate-range

Family

- ➢ Long-range
- ➢ Intermediate-range
- ➢ Short-range
- ➢ Immediate-range

Community

- ➢ Long-range
- ➢ Intermediate-range
- ➢ Short-range
- ➢ Immediate-range

Professional

- ➢ Long-range
- ➢ Intermediate-range
- ➢ Short-range
- ➢ Immediate-range

Physical

- ➢ Long-range
- ➢ Intermediate-range
- ➢ Short-range
- ➢ Immediate-range

Personal Growth

- ➢ Long-range
- ➢ Intermediate-range
- ➢ Short-range
- ➢ Immediate-range

Strategy

> ➤ Knowledge
> ➤ Skills
> ➤ Attitude
> ➤ Resources
> ➤ Empowerment
> ➤ Processes

Mighty Mentors:
Your Personal Board of Directors

One of the best things you can do for yourself is to recruit a personal "board of directors." Your board will be made up of people who know you well and who will make it their business to help you succeed.

After I attended Coach Joe's seminar, I took the opportunity to get to know him, and we became very good friends. I watch Joe speak every opportunity I get. He never ceases to amaze me with his energy and the way he leads his professional life.

Joe became my "speaking" mentor in 2002. When we get together each month, I tell him what is going on in my career, and he provides invaluable guidance and support. Since Joe became my speaking mentor, my speaking career has really taken off. I am much more effective, confident, and dynamic. I'm also more willing to take risks, trying new things that I never would have had the courage to try before Joe became my mentor. My business has increased more than tenfold, and my income has more than doubled. Joe is an awesome mentor and an incredible friend.

Recruiting your "Board"

It did not stop there. My experience with Joe was so important that I added mentors (or board members) to help in the financial, spiritual, family and community areas of my life. I call my team of mentors my "Board of Directors." Just like a Board of Directors for a corporation, my Board guides me toward greater growth, development and achievement. I believe every person can benefit from forming a personal "Board."

As you think about potential Board members, choose carefully. Next to your family members, these people will have more influence on your life than anyone else. Make sure they are outstanding in the area you want them to mentor you in. They should be people you want to imitate and learn from. You will be asking them to provide you with guidance, encouragement, and correction, and to hold you accountable. You'll ask them to answer your questions to the best of their ability and to celebrate with you when you succeed.

Use the spaces below to brainstorm some potential mentors. As you recruit them, make sure they understand what you are requesting of them (see preceding paragraph). It's an honor to serve as a board member, but it's also a lot of work!

Your Board of Directors

Financial Mentor _____

Professional Mentor _____

Spiritual Mentor _____

Family Mentor _____

Community Mentor _____

Physical Mentor _____

Personal Growth Mentor _____

Leisure Mentor _____

Developing your board of directors will help you in two important ways. First, you'll be surrounded with people who share a passion for your success. Second, you'll have wonderful models for all the abilities you want to develop in your own life.

Awesome! Now, make the calls. Make it a big deal. Let each mentor that you recruit know how much you respect them and value their expertise. If some of your recruits aren't able to serve as your mentor, start brainstorming another person who would be just as capable. It's always better to have someone who will be committed 100%.

Try Something New

"Think left and think right and think low and think high. Oh, the thinks you can think up if only you try."
                                        --Dr. Seuss

In his book, *How to Stop Worrying and Start Living*, Dale Carnegie says that 99% of the things we worry about never happen. In fact, he tells a story of a man who wrote down his problems and put them away in his desk for thirty days. After the thirty days had passed, he reread the things he had written down, and none of them had happened.

In his book, *The 4 Hour Work Week*, Tim Ferriss talks about doing the big things in life. Most of the competition is in doing the mundane stuff. Most people are scared, so they do not want to take risks or try new things. If you want to make a big splash, try something big. It is easier to do than the mundane and more rewarding. You can fail at either one, so go for something big.

The point of these two authors is this: Most people don't live the life for which they were designed, because they never stop thinking about all of the small, scary stuff that is never going to happen. Instead, you should focus on the big stuff that pushes you out of your comfort zone. When you tackle the big stuff, you will not only make a difference, you will feel awesome about yourself.

Set yourself up to succeed. You can do anything you set your mind to, if you will only establish your vision and put your action plan in place behind it! Now that you know yourself a little better, what are the things in life that you were designed to do? What are the things that you have always wanted to do but haven't done?

Your Perfect Job

All of us dream of finding the perfect job. Imagine looking forward to going to work, feeling confident all day long, and heading home happy and fulfilled at the end of the day. For each of us, there's a perfect job that will best help us realize

Additional Ideas Available Online
embraceyourfreakness.com

our personal vision. Think about all the variables of a job, and answer the questions below to help you imagine your perfect job.

> What specific activities would you do in a typical day? (Be as specific as possible.)

> Where would you work? Inside? Outdoors? At home?

> Would you work alone or would you be part of a team?

> What would the other people you work with be like?

> What responsibilities would you have?

> What hours would you work?

> What is the one thing you would have to do in this job that you really wouldn't like doing?

> Who would your customers be? Who would you serve daily?

Now put it all together and write a paragraph describing your perfect job.

Job Description:

Does the job you've described exist? If not, could you create it? What would it take for you to get paid for doing what you love to do?

Your Perfect Life

The perfect job is one thing, but life is more than just working. Because most of us spend most of our waking time working, we focused on the perfect job first. Now that you have a handle on that part of your life, let's branch out to the rest of your life.

Remember back in the goals section of the book? You took the balanced life inventory. Your pie graph showed you at a glance how well-balanced your life is right now.

It's time to dream for a moment. You see, goals are simply dreams with deadlines and plans. If you cannot see it, you cannot achieve it. Let's take a moment and visualize, which is just a fancy way of saying, let's dream.

Dreams are one of life's best motivators. Without dreams, life would be very dreary. So let's program some of our dreams, by purposely creating them, writing them down and repeating them every day for 30 days. This will implant those dreams in your subconscious mind, then your mind will go to work making those dreams happen in your life.

So here's your chance to envision your Perfect Dream Life:

- ➢ Where would you live?

- ➢ How would you spend your time and energy?

- ➢ Who would you be of service to? What people would you help get what they want/need?
- ➢ Who would be in your life?

- ➢ Who would your friends be?

➤ Who would your family be?

➤ What would your daily activities look like?

➤ What would the weather be like?

➤ What time would you rise? What time would you go to bed?

➤ What would you eat for your meals?

➤ What would you be like from a physical perspective? Would you be slim, bulky, athletic, soft, firm, youthful, tan, healthy, vibrant, lanky, etc.?

➤ What would your personality be like? Laid back, go-getter, people person, detail oriented, etc.?

➤ Ask your own questions. Come up with your own life details.

Now put it all together and write a paragraph describing your perfect life.

Life Description:

Getting "There"

You now know where "there" is. You've identified that "one thing" that your life is all about. Now it's time to go out and start your new and improved life. Read over your Job Description and your Life Description first thing in the morning and again in the evening before you go to bed. Engrave them on your heart and mind and soul. Set your sights on making your vision for your life a reality. Work past the obstacles and concentrate on achieving your goals.

Telling the World

"And will you succeed? Yes! You will indeed! (98 and ¾ percent guaranteed.)"

--Dr. Seuss

You're finally ready to tell the world about your Freakness. Fortunately, this is a fairly simple process:

Step 1: Find someone.
Step 2: Share your Freakness.
Step 3: Ask them to share theirs.
That's pretty simple, right? But what do you say, and how do you say it? Read on, my freaky friend!

Your Elevator Speech

During the economic boom of the 1990s, venture capitalists heard from a lot of would-be entrepreneurs in search of

**Elevator Speech Ideas
Available Online**
embraceyourfreakness.com

cash. Many times, the entrepreneurs only had the length of the elevator ride to sell their ideas. The brief, punchy, persuasive speeches they used during those elevator rides came to be known as elevator speeches. Now it's time for you to write an elevator speech to tell people who you are and what you're all about—in three minutes or less.

The good news is that all the exercises you've worked through in this book will give you all the information you need to write your elevator speech. Make sure you include the following things:

1) Who are you? (Your name)

2) What are you all about? (Your vision statement)

3) How are you going to make your vision a reality? (Your mission statement)

4) What three critical factors will make you successful in your journey? (List three of your greatest strengths.)

Now write it down, practice it out loud, practice it on your dog, and then practice it on your friends. If you really want to feel confident, practice it on your friends' dogs. Practice it until you know it backwards and forwards and until you can deliver it with grace and confidence in any place, at any time.

My Elevator Speech

Key Points

What have you learned about your life's purpose?

What have you learned about the self-discovery process?

How can you help others in this pursuit of our true selves? Based on what you have learned, what kinds of things are you best suited to do well? (Look back at the perfect job description you already wrote.)

3. Take Care:
Keeping the Freakness Fresh

"A mind that has been stretched will never return to its original dimension."

--Albert Einstein

I In the first chapter of this book, you looked inward to learn what you're made of, to discover your Freakness. That process involved taking inventory of all the wonderful and varied ingredients that have gone into making you a unique and remarkable human being.

In the second chapter you looked outward at the world to figure out where you wanted your life to be headed. You figured out how to embrace your Freakness and to use it to live out your life's purpose. You learned how to begin the journey toward living the successful, fulfilling life you were designed to live.

Now that you know those two things, it's time to focus on how to program your brain to handle all the challenges, failures and successes that are sure to come your way as you journey toward your destination. Make no mistake about it, the road is full of all three.

Programming Your Brain

The key to successfully traveling life's rocky road is learning to see obstacles not as barriers to success, but as opportunities for learning. To do that, you need to change your mindset. Changing mindset takes mental aerobics, calisthenics for the cranium, mind molding. If you can learn to see challenges as opportunities, you can use them to propel you forward rather than letting them stop you in your tracks.

You have spent a considerable amount of time taking your inventory and crafting your personal vision and mission. You know your Freakness, and you're determined to make it work for you. How do you keep the razor sharp? How do you keep your engine fine-tuned? Now that you are a well- oiled machine, outside forces will try to take you down, making you feel inferior, clouding your focus. This chapter will help you develop the mental fortitude to deal with anything that life throws in your path.

Your Personal 80/20 Rule

In Marcus Buckingham's video series, "Now, Discover Your Strengths," Buckingham talks about how many people make the mistake of concentrating on improving their weaknesses instead of developing their strengths. Of course we have to pay attention to our weaknesses, but Buckingham argues that building up our strengths is much more important. He suggests incorporating Pareto's Principle of Self-development, which says that 80% of your personal development energy should be dedicated to improving your strengths, with the remaining 20% dedicated to improving your weaknesses. Employing this 80/20 principle in your own life will increase your self-confidence dramatically, by helping you get better at the things you're already good at and that you probably enjoy doing. It also prevents you from spinning your wheels, wasting valuable time working on that one thing you just can't seem to master. Based on the 80/20 rule, you should delegate things you're not good at to others on your team—colleagues, family members, etc. That way you don't have to get bogged down doing things you're not suited to do, yet the work will still get done.

Changing Your Inner Voice

Charlie "Tremendous" Jones was one of my favorite speakers. Charlie said that tomorrow you will become what you think about today. It's the old garbage in-garbage out scenario. If you put negative stuff in your brain, you will get negative stuff out of your brain. By contrast, if you put quality stuff in your brain, you will reap the benefits in an improved quality of life.

This chapter is all about feeding your brain, so we'll be thinking carefully about what makes good brain food, good skull candy. We'll look at some simple tools that will boost your self-confidence and greatly increase your ability to accomplish anything you set out to achieve. It takes dedication. Feeding your brain is kind of like taking a shower, you have to take one every day or the freshness wears off, and you start to feel stale and sluggish. By contrast, the more often you feed your brain positive inputs, the more power your brain has to get things done.

It's all about changing your inner voice, your internal dialog. It's about replacing the negative messages you're feeding yourself with positive, ego-building offerings. In order to help you be intentional about this process, I've developed an easy-to-use system. I call my system of positive mental inputs SNAPS.

SNAPS

SNAPS stands for **Sub-Neuro Achievement Production System.** This is my systematic program for feeding your brain positive statements about things you'd like to be or that you'd like to accomplish. The secret is to phrase these statements not as wishes for the future, but as statements of fact, as objective realities. In response, your brain will accept these statements as truths and go about making them happen. Remember that SNAPS must be written in the present tense and stated positively. Take a look at some sample SNAPS below:

I am an excellent and exceptional person.
    (Courtesy of Coach Joe Gilliam)
I am a winner.
People like and respect me.
I am a loved and respected person in my community.
I make $100,000 per year.
I have a loving, caring, and honorable family.
I am successful in all the things I do.
I am worthy of success.
I have an attitude of servitude.

Try writing ten SNAPs of your own:

1.	6.
2.	7.
3.	8.
4.	9.
5.	10.

SNAPS are a great way of programming your mind for success. They are a no-cost investment in helping you become what you want to become. Repeat your ten SNAPS to yourself twice a day for 30 days and see what miracles you achieve in your life.

PEARLS

As powerful as SNAPS are, they're only half the equation when it comes to programming your mind for fulfillment. The other half consists of PEARLS: not the tiny natural objects that amaze us with their perfection, but **P**ersonal **E**nduring **A**ttribute **R**ealization **L**etters that you'll collect from ten people who know you well and can enumerate all your wonderful qualities. In the business world, when a company does a good job, they ask for a referral letter from their satisfied client. Your goal will be to collect ten pearls from people who can provide positive feedback for you.

The PEARL concept came to me from a friend of mine more than 20 years ago. We were taking a class together, and he wrote down on a 3x5 index card a short note that told me of a strength he saw in me and how that made a difference in his life. I thought it was really terrific. As a matter of fact, I still have that 3x5 index card today.

So I started writing similar notes for people I know when I wanted to show some appreciation, or just to let them know that their strengths were being recognized. After writing these notes for a while, I thought of the acronym PEARL and started teaching it in my seminars.

So when you want to give someone a PEARL, write down a Positive Enduring Attribute. Tell that person about a strength you see in them that is making a positive difference, no matter how big or small, in the world. You can write down your PEARL on a 3x5 index card, on a sticky note, or in the form of a letter. It does not have to be fancy–sometimes just a line or two–or, at most, a paragraph will do. As a rule, I try to focus my PEARLs on just one specific strength.

Giving PEARLs is easy, but how do you get people to give you PEARLS? There are a few ways to get them. Most simply, you can ask for them. Explain the concept, and then ask those closest to you to write you one. People who care about you are usually glad for the chance to build you up.

Second, start writing them for other people. As you start sharing PEARLs, they will certainly come back to you. As the old Bible saying goes, "whatsoever a man soweth, that shall he also reap." It may take you a while to get 10 PEARLs, but this isn't a race, it's a marathon. I would predict that for every 25 PEARLs you give, you will get at least one in return. That's a pretty good return on your investment.

One final thing about PEARLS, they have to be sincere. The worst thing to do is to be insincere with your PEARLs. People recognize insincerity a mile away, and then you have not put out a Positive Enduring Attribute Recognition Letter, you have put out a SIN—Seemingly Insincere News.

Once you've collected your PEARLS, keep them close at hand and read them on a regular basis. As new people come into your life, update your PEARLS and set a goal of adding one per month to keep them fresh and relevant. How will you think differently about yourself with positive feedback coming at you on a consistent basis? I have no doubt that it will help change your life!

Picking Positive Influencers

"You become like the five people you spend the most time with."
--Charlie "Tremendous" Jones

So I worked on my SNAPS every day and got eleven PEARLs from eleven people I respected. It was amazing! The combined impact of changing my own internal dialog and bombarding myself with positive information from others absolutely transformed how I felt about myself.

Then I decided to take it to the next level: I started hanging out with people who truly liked themselves, people who wanted to accomplish things in life, rather than people who were going backwards, or simply drifting. And, guess what happened? I too became more positive, more focused, and truly eager to accomplish my goals.

I also noticed that I was happier. I was making new friends, getting more done, making more money, and, something I hadn't expected, helping more people! People were actually seeking out my advice and learning from me. I was becoming a mentor. Not only was my own life changing for the better, but I was helping others change their lives for the better as well!

Charlie was right. Each of us is a product not only of the experiences we have, the books we read, and the videos we watch, but the people we hang out with. As you work toward actualizing your personal vision, I suggest that you examine each of these areas independently. You may find out, as I did, that you have quite a bit of negativity in your life that you can do something about.

When you meet new people, always ask yourself, "What are their strengths?" and "What can I learn from them?" You will be amazed at the wide range of strengths others have and how they can help you to become even more incredible than you already are. Instead of taking away from your uniqueness, focusing on the positive things others can teach you will help you fully embrace your Freakness. Personal benchmarking is a tool that not only helps you look for good things in others; it also helps you remember to focus on the good things in yourself.

Personal Benchmarking

Personal Benchmarking is all about personal innovation. Don't feel like you have to reinvent the wheel. Take the wheel that someone else made and make it better. Change it to work for you. Massage it, make subtle changes, make it fit your life and your personality. Keep in mind that you shouldn't expect to be able to develop all the attributes you see in others. You have to pick and choose those that suit you best.

So take a minute and think about five different people that you know and respect in your life. For each person, think of one quality that you see in them that you'd like to see more of in yourself, and list them here:

1.
2.
3.
4.
5.

Now think of five more people you admire but that you don't know personally. For each of these five, think of an attribute that you admire in them and that you'd like to work on developing in yourself. List those five things here:

6.
7.
8.
9.
10.

Your Personal Filters

"If you really want to do something, you'll find a way; if you don't, you'll find an excuse."

--Jim Rohn

Filters—they control how we see life. But the good news is that we control our filters. How do you view life? Is your glass half full, or is it half empty? Are you grateful for what you have, or are you always wanting more? Are you genuinely happy in life? If not, why not? If you are happy, what makes you content and fulfilled?

Abraham Lincoln said, "People are about as happy as they make up their minds to be." There is a lot of truth to that statement. Make up your mind to be happy. Go make someone's day by giving them a PEARL.

Anchoring

Anchoring is a powerful tool that can change your frame of mind in an instant. Imagine yourself in a stressful interview, under pressure to answer a question just the way the employer wants, to give just the right example from your experiences to convince the interviewer that you're the employee they've been waiting to hire. Wouldn't it be wonderful to have an easy way to instantly put yourself in an emotional state where you're feeling your absolute best?

In order to get a sense of how Anchoring works, think back to a great moment in your life. Perhaps it was your graduation, your wedding day, the birth of a child, or the day you achieved a great milestone or received a well-deserved award. Whatever your moment was, write it down. Describe who was there; recount the events of the day in as much detail as you can remember. Include the emotions you felt, the sounds you heard, the smells you smelled. Be as expansive as possible. Write it down with the goal of enabling yourself to relive the experience. The more detail you can recall in your retelling, the better the anchor will work:

_____

_____

_____

_____

_____

Wonderful! I hope you have captured your moment in enough detail that you can really relive it. Now I'll use an example from one of the great moments in my life to show you how to connect your great moment to a physical gesture that will bring all the wonderful emotion of your moment back to you whenever you need it most.

I proposed to my wife Rachel on December 30, 2007, at my parents' home in Bonita Springs, Florida. My mom and dad and Rachel and I were seated at the dinner table. It was a beautiful evening, about 65 degrees with a slight breeze.

Dad knew I was going to propose, but Mom and Rachel did not. As we finished the soup, I turned to my dad and said, "You know, Pop, I have been looking for my soul twin for my entire life, and now I've found her." Then I turned to Rachel and pulled out the ring and grabbed her hand and asked her to be my soul twin forever. My heart was racing, my palms were sweaty; I was so excited! As soon as I had turned to Rachel, Dad had whipped out the digital camera, so he got everything on film.

I wish you could have seen Rachel. She was radiant, absolutely beaming with that smile that is hers alone. I will never forget how I felt when she said, "Yes," and agreed to marry me. I was the happiest I have ever been. I knew God had helped me find my soul twin, and we would be together forever. I looked over at my mother who was battling cancer and she had this big 'ole grin. She was so happy for us! Having Mom healthy enough to share our joy was the icing on the cake.

Now, whenever I touch the inside of my wedding ring with my left thumb, I go right back to that moment when I proposed, with all the wonderful images, emotions, and energy that made it a highpoint in my life. To anchor the moment, I relived it over and over in my mind, in vivid detail, each time touching my wedding ring with my left thumb. After about 21 times, the movement became inextricably attached to the feelings. Now I have at my fingertips an instant change of mental attitude—very cool stuff indeed!

Anchoring works because the human brain can have only one thought or emotion at a time; two contradictory emotions cannot co-exist. Therefore, if you can successfully tie a positive emotion to a physical motion or gesture, like touching your wedding ring, you have a powerful tool for banishing negative emotions. You can instantly call up positive feelings whenever you need a boost!

If you're not convinced of the power of anchoring, just think a little bit about your own negative anchors. Say you've been yelled at by your boss day in and day out for months on end. Isn't the sound of your boss's footsteps coming down the hall enough to tie your stomach in knots?

Instead of letting negative anchors control your responses, create some positive anchors for yourself so that you can draw on their power whenever you need it. Anchoring lets you take control of your mental attitude instead of letting negative feelings control you.

Getting a Mental Check up

Imagine yourself reading over your SNAPS every day, getting fresh PEARLS regularly, accessing your best moments through anchoring, and hanging out with positive people who you want to emulate in your life. Would you believe me if I told you your life still had areas of negativity? I didn't believe it until I attended a seminar with Coach Joe Gilliam, a master motivator. Coach Joe convinced me that I still had areas of negativity that I needed to eliminate from my life.

Have you ever had a "moment of realization?" In February of 2001, I had such a moment during a seminar with Coach Joe. Joe told me (and the other seminar participants) that we wouldn't be at our most productive and most positive unless we eliminated the negative influences we were choosing to input into our computers (our brains) every day.

Now, I thought, "Negative influences, not me. No way. I've chosen to surround myself with positive, supportive people." But Joe went on to ask, "In the last 30 days, how many of you have watched television? How many of you have listened to the radio? How many of you have read the newspaper or the news on the internet?" Ouch. He had me. I was three for three on those criteria. I watched TV every day, listened to the radio in my car, and made a point of keeping up with the news either via the newspaper or the internet. I knew I was in good company when Joe said, "All of you raised your hands."

Now, for Joe, our unanimous response was telling, and it told him two things in particular. First, it told him that all of us had time to put information into our brains. Second, it told him that despite being people who wanted to improve our own lives and make a difference in the world, we were choosing to input negative information a large percentage of the time.

Joe continued, "How many of you in the last 30 days have read a motivational or self improvement book?" About 25% of the hands went up. "In the last 30 days, how many of you have listened to a motivational audio or video program?" Only about 10% of the hands were raised.

After that, Joe's conclusion was inescapable: How could we expect to become more positive and effective when we were spending so much of our energy loading our mental computers with viruses and junk mail?

Does this mean we should never watch television, listen to the radio or read the paper? Of course not. But it does mean we need to choose to consciously put positive information into our brains to counterbalance all of the negative stimuli that we receive all day, every day, just by living in the world.

Joe is right. Zig is right. Charlie is right. The people who are the happiest and who accomplish the most in life are the people that choose to put positive information into their brains. You cannot input negative information and negative emotion and expect to accomplish anything. The brain does not work that way.

Are you willing to do what it takes to input positive information? It's time for "a check up from the neck up" as Zig Ziglar would say.

Your check up:

In the last 30 days, have you watched television?

In the last 30 days, have you listened to the radio?

In the last 30 days, have you read the newspaper?

In the last 30 days, have you read a motivational or self-improvement book?

In the last 30 days, have you listened to or watched a motivational or self-improvement audio or video program?